Guidance in Your Handbag

100 Thoughts to Inspire You Every Day

Prabha Srinivasan

BALBOA.
PRESS
A DIVISION OF HAY HOUSE

Author Credits: Holistic Life Coach

Balboa Press books may be ordered through booksellers or by contacting:

Balboa Press
A Division of Hay House
1663 Liberty Drive
Bloomington, IN 47403
www.balboapress.com.au
1 (877) 407-4847

Print information available on the last page.

ISBN: 978-1-5043-0440-5 (sc)
ISBN: 978-1-5043-0441-2 (e)

Balboa Press rev. date: 09/21/2016

Acknowledgement

I dedicate this book to all the wonderful people who have had a positive effect on my life, when I needed it the most.

I would like to make a special mention of thanks to my mother, Usha, who planted the seed of service in my mind. *No amount of words can express my gratitude for all that you have done for me. All my services are dedicated to you, amma.*

Special thanks to Krupa Balgi for making this book happen.

Praise for Guidance in your Handbag:

"This guide founded on heartfelt insights immediately speaks to you. Each impression, shines a light that deepens one's self-awareness, ignites a sense of inner strength, and awakens a knowing from deep within. These honest, and authentic insights, genuinely sooth the soul, and enliven ones being with clarity and confidence."

– Michelle Black MCNS, GCCM.
   Founding Director of ELEGROW

Introduction

The thoughts published in this book are insights that I have received during my daily meditation. I use meditation as a tool to receive guidance and in(ner)tuitions that add clarity to my thinking. When you read the thoughts in this book, I request you to bear in mind that these insights were addressed to me from my higher consciousness. While they can be relevant to you, these thoughts are not my preaching to you in any way. They simply are thoughts that showed up in my consciousness, and I felt that they may be of use to more than just me. Hence this book.

It is my deepest desire that this book provide you with messages of hope, clarity, and positive thinking. If this book can soothe your soul just once, that will be my wish fulfilled.

Recommendation for using this book:

I encourage you to use this book like a first-aid kit. When you find yourself spiralling down with a negative thought or a situation, open this book to a random page, and contemplate on the thought that you see on the page. Do this exercise every time you find yourself in stress to help you snap out of negative thought patterns and redirect your thinking to a more positive and promising path. Whichever page you open, know that it contains a special message for you.

Additional exercise:

To get the full benefit of the messages in this book, I recommend you keep a journal and write in it each day regarding what that day's message means to you and how it is relevant to your current situation. Date these journal entries, and regularly read back to your past entries. This will give you a deeper understanding of your life and your journey forward.

More information:

Guidance in Your Handbag is also available as an app for smart phone. To download the app, visit Google Play Store and search for 'shftinside'. If you would like help with meditation, or journaling, or if you would like to know more about my services, you can visit my website: www.shftinside. com. You can also send me a personal message through the website, and I will be pleased to connect with you.

1 Depth

You are deeper than the thoughts you have.

2 *Self-worth*

Every experience in life comes down to one thing:
how you feel about yourself.

3 Balance

Life is a dance between doing and being. You cannot appreciate one without the other.

4 Now

When your focus stays in the present moment, you exercise free will. Until then, you are bound by your fears and anxieties. **Free will only exists in the now.**

5 Reflection

Everything you see in others, you have within yourself - good, bad, and ugly!

6 Let go

The purpose of all practise is to increase your confidence to such an extent that you can finally let go of control.

7 *Viewpoint*

Life situations occur, so you can start to see yourself differently.

8 The path

Focusing your awareness on the heart gently opens up a pathway to your inner sanctuary.

9 Clarity

When you connect with yourself, you get clear on what truly matters to you.

10 Inner peace

Living in peace with yourself can heal all of your ailments, at every level of your being.

11 All is well

*At the centre of your being, **all is well**, all the time.*

12 *Voluntary*

Life is like a simulated video game. You put yourself in situations voluntarily to undertake experiential learning.

13 *Love*

To love is to radiate your beauty, warmth, and glow from the core of your being out towards everything and everyone around you.

14 *Connect*

Your heart is your internal mirror. It reflects to you all aspects of yourself. Take time to connect and look within.

15 *Grandness*

Every struggle, every confusion, and every mess you find yourself in has been intricately designed so that you can call forth a grander version of yourself from within.

16 *Promise*

Everything you have today was your longing not long ago, and everything you are longing for now is coming - not long to go.

17 Life

Things get created in order to be destroyed. Things get destroyed in order to be re-created. This is the process of life.

18 *Strength*

Moving forward consists of small, steady steps, while refining and strengthening your moves to get ready for the big leap.

19 *Faith*

When life takes over, follow it faithfully; it will escort you to a higher road.

20 Fulfilment

Don't worry about the road ahead. Focus on the next step, and take this step with all the grace and reverence you can possibly demonstrate. **Fulfilment is hidden in your next step.**

21 *Thoughts*

Every thought matters; every thought manifests.

22 *Guidance*

Guidance is always flowing into your awareness, whether you notice it or not.

23 *Acceptance*

Acceptance leads to appreciation. Appreciation leads to freedom. If you want to be free, first accept everything in your life as it is, and trust that it will result in betterment.

24 Self-reliance

Be your own rock.

25 *Faith*

Faith is the unshakeable knowing that life is good, no matter how this present moment appears to be.

26 Drop the fight

When you learn to accept your own flaws, you learn to accept other people's flaws. When you are fighting for perfection in yourself, you are also fighting for perfection in everyone else.

27 *Actions*

Let nothing you do determine how you feel. Determine how you want to feel, feel it, and then do.

28 Centre

There is a deep sense of calm and quietness within you that is undisturbed by external circumstances. This is your centre.

29 Withdraw

When life gives you too much to handle, withdraw into your centre. Stay here as long and as often as you need, to find your inner-strength.

30 Flow

Drop your resistance and go with the flow. All of your desires will be met.

31 Desires

Honour your desires. Suppressed desires crave gratification and override your intentions.

32 Shift

Your mind is constantly trying to categorise things and put them in boxes. And yet there are things that cannot be categorised. This is when you get called to shift from the head to heart.

33 *Release*

Release the urge to own people in your life. Move into a much freer space known as co-existence.

34 *Love*

Come back to love.

35 Higher Purpose

There is nothing unsacred in this world. Even what you consider the worst action or the worst thought, leads to a higher purpose.

36 Gifts

Spiritual unfoldment is the process of opening the inner gifts that have been with you all your life.

37 Results

Success and failure are not exclusive. Success in one field implies failure in another. Failure in one field implies success in another.

38 Inspired action

Follow your inner nudge. Put yourself out in the world. And know that your job finishes there. Results are not your concern.

39 Perfection

You were not born to experience a perfect life. You were born to experience the perfection embedded in a seemingly imperfect life.

40 *Authority*

Everything starts with you and ends with you.
The you who is invisible, intangible, and buried
deep inside your being.

41 Creation

Life is not a competition. Life is a collaborative creation.

42 *Illusion*

Your mind has the ability to take something temporary (pain or pleasure) and make it seem eternal.

43 Partnership

When you attempt to control, you block your own expansion. Replace control with partnership.

44 Seek help

You don't have to do it alone.

45 Service

Focus on your service.

46 *Joy*

Your consciousness is constantly striving for expansion. When you block the expansion, you experience stress. When you allow it, you experience joy.

47 *Life*

Have faith in the process of life.

48 *Strive*

It is human to feel negative. It is also human to strive for the positive.

49 *Reality*

Reality begins with a thought.

50 *Wake up*

Every obstacle on your path is a wake-up call to remember your true strength.

51 Influence

As you open your heart and reach for that which is beyond the physical, you create ripples of energy around you calling forth others to do the same.

52 *Freedom*

When you meditate, you free yourself to fly high into the realm of pure positivity.

53 Re(in)novate

Things (and relationships) break down so they can be rebuilt with more understanding, more passion, and larger purpose.

54 Knowing

Underneath all of your confusion, there is clarity -
a clear knowing of the way forward.

55 *Answer*

Love is the answer to all your questions. Be love.
Breathe love. Give love.

56 Flexibility

The only way to move beyond life's setbacks is to allow them to shape you.

57 *Stretch*

You were not born to live in comfort zone.

58 Power of choice

When you are fighting with your current reality,
you lose your power to choose.

59 Beauty

The things that you declare as ugly are like the emission tube in an automobile - when you see the big picture, you can appreciate the beauty in the ugliness.

60 *Reach out*

You are not alone. There are many others going through the same journey as you. Reach out and connect.

61 *Heal*

When you heal yourself, you heal others. When you help others heal, you heal yourself.

62 *Peace*

Peace is not the absence of struggles. Peace is the end result of struggles.

63 Gather yourself

Feeling loved is feeling together with yourself.

64 Decision

Your decision only decides your journey, not your destination. Your destination remains the same no matter what you decide.

65 *Destination*

Your life's destination is to open up your awareness to the totality of your being.

66 Time

You have plenty of time. There is no need to rush.

67 *Possibility*

Stepping out of your current life and exploring a grander version of yourself involves opening your mind to new possibilities.

68 *Ever present*

Human body can only be present at a specific time and place. The soul, however is ever present, unrestricted by time, and space. To tune into your ever present nature cut down physical activities, and sit quietly in meditation.

69 *Choose*

Accept all thoughts (without questioning), but choose which ones to act on.

70 *Mystery*

You don't have to figure it all out. Some things are better left as mystery to unfold at the appropriate time.

71 *Faith*

Hope is staying open to new possibilities. Faith is knowing that one of those possibilities will lead you to your end goal.

72 *Clarity*

Embrace your confusion. It is a necessary step to clarity.

73 Change

Nothing in this world can cause you misery except your thoughts. Change your thoughts - end your misery.

74 *Purpose*

There is divine order behind all your actions. Even if they seem chaotic, they are leading you to your soul's purpose.

75 *Allow*

Every time you let go of something, you allow something new to come to you.

76 Challenges

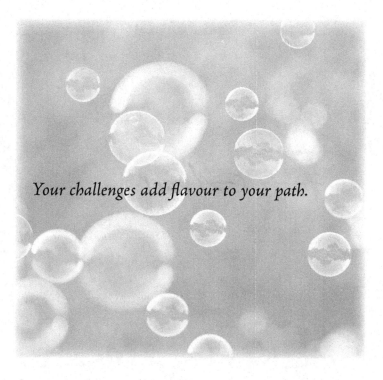

Your challenges add flavour to your path.

77 Angel

Find the angel in you to comfort you, to hold your hand, and lead you in times of stress.

78 Soul agenda

*All suffering endured serve the soul's agenda.
When it stops serving you, you will find a way
to end it.*

79 Experiment

Life is an ongoing experiment. Negative results teach you more than positive results.

80 Growth

Your spiritual awareness is like a blade of grass: growing at a steady pace, no matter what.

81 *Determination*

You are always at an intersection between something old and something new. Which way you go depends on your determination.

82 Creative Energy

Creative energy is always flowing to you like a beam of light. When you are relaxed, light, or calm you feel it's presence. When you clouded, dense, or dark, you are disconnected from it.

83 *Self-doubt*

Self-doubt is rooted in grief. What shows up as self-doubt is, in essence, grief of losing the old self.

84 Truth

Your self-worth is not defined by your failures, or your success. Your self-worth is shaped by you being true to yourself.

85 *Companion*

When you begin your conscious inner journey guidance may trickle or appear random. With time they become a companion you can count on.

86 *Future*

Your desired future is already here - sneaking into your life when you are not looking.

87 *Conflict*

Some conflicts are about resolution. Some conflicts are about learning to express without guilt.

88 *Awareness*

Everyday adds a drop to the ocean of your awareness.

89 Ask

If you had complete faith in yourself and the world (to support you), what would you ask for?

90 Coincidence

All coincidences have a meaning. The meaning is that you are important.

91 Possibilities

All possibilities exist within you. You are using your thoughts to choose and bring into experience the one possibility that matches your thinking.

92 *Luck*

When you live your life unconsciously, unaware of your creative power, you experience fate. When you live your life consciously, owning your creative power, you experience luck.

93 Growth

Focus on your growth. When you grow the world grows.

94 Manifestation

No two manifestations are the same, even if they relate to similar goal. The process will vary each time. Enjoy the difference. Allow it to expand you.

95 *Nature*

It is alright to be all over the place! That is the nature of your Soul.

96 Energy

You are the energy that runs the machine called your body.

97 Boundless

There is no boundary to where you start and the universal energy ends. You are it - like a drop in the ocean.

98 Contrast

What is unlike you helps you know what is like you.

99 Fear

Love your fears. They show you the direction for your expansion.

100 Peace

What thoughts can you think now to make yourself feel peaceful?

Printed in the United States
By Bookmasters